KU-113-051

MEAN MACHINES
SPORTS CARS

CHRIS OXLADE

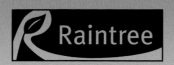

www.raintreepublishers.co.uk
Visit our website to find out more information about **Raintree** books.

To order:
 Phone 44 (0) 1865 888113
 Send a fax to 44 (0) 1865 314091
Visit the Raintree Bookshop at **www.raintreepublishers.co.uk** to browse our catalogue and order online.

First published in Great Britain by
Raintree, Halley Court,
Jordan Hill, Oxford OX2 8EJ, part of
Harcourt Education.
Raintree is a registered trademark of
Harcourt Education Ltd.

Editorial: Diyan Leake and Rachel Tisdale
Design: Michelle Lisseter and Keith Williams
Picture Research: Rachel Tisdale
Production: Jonathan Smith
Illustrations: Keith Williams and Peter Bull

Originated by Ambassador Litho Ltd
Printed and bound in Hong Kong,
China by South China Printing Company

ISBN 1 844 43171 1
09 08 07 06 05
10 9 8 7 6 5 4 3 2 1

British Library Cataloguing in Publication Data
Oxlade, Chris
Sports Cars – (Mean Machines)
I.Title
629.2'221
A full catalogue record for this book is available from
the British Library.

Acknowledgements
Alvey & Towers Picture Library: p. **31**; Aston Martin:
title page, pp. **5, 35** (t); BMW: pp. **11** (t), **23**; Bob
Masters Photography: p. **32** (t); Bugatti: p. **57** (b);
Chrysler: pp. **5** (t,r), **8** (b), **9** (b), **16, 21, 27** (t), **43** (t),
57 (t); Corbis: pp. **6** (b) (Richard Olivier), **9** (t)
(Andrew DeMattos), **10** (t) (Pitchal FR), **13** (b) (Alain
Denize), **14** (World Racing Images), **24** (l) (George D.
Lepp), **28** (Vittoriano Rastelli), **34** (Ben Wood), **35** (b)
(Joseph Sohm/ChromoSohm Inc.), **36** (Kim Sayer), **40**
(l) (Cy Jariz Cyrl/NewSport), **41** (t) (Alan Schein
Photography), **45** (b) (Jean-Francois Galeron/World
Racing Images), **48** (Joseph Sohm/ChromoSohm Inc.),
49 (t) (Hulton-Deutsch Collection), **49** (b) (Robert
Dowling), **50** (David Lees), **51** (t) (George D. Lepp),
52 (t) (Bettmann), **52** (b) (Ted Soqui), **53** (t) (Joseph
Sohm/ChromoSohm Inc.), **53** (b) (Ted Soqui), **54** (t)
(Bettmann), **56** (Ted Soqui); Corbis Sygma: pp. **46** (t)
(Bembaron Jeremy), **51** (b) (Nogues Alain); Ford: p. **6**
(t); Honda: pp. **12–13** (t); Mazda: pp. **8** (l), **10, 11, 26**;
Mercedes: pp. **29, 39** (t); Morgan Motor Company: p.
37 (b); Neill Bruce: pp. **25** (t), **30, 32** (b), **33, 37** (t);
Noble Automotive Limited: pp. **18** (b), **19** (b);
Peugeot Sport UK: pp. **17** (r), **26** (t), **38, 39** (b), **44, 45**
(t), **46** (b), **47**; Porsche: pp. **4, 5** (m,r), **16, 17, 22, 42,
43** (b), **54** (b), **55**; Tim Skipper/www.sports190.com:
p. **15**; TVR: pp. **19** (t), **24** (b), **25** (b).

Cover photograph of a Ferrari F50 convertible
reproduced with permission of Alvey & Towers
Picture Library

The publishers would like to thank Dr J. Knezevic for
his assistance in the preparation of this book.

Disclaimer
All the Internet addresses (URLs) given in this book
were valid at the time of going to press. However, due
to the dynamic nature of the Internet, some addresses
may have changed, or sites may have changed or
ceased to exist since publication. While the author and
publisher regret any inconvenience this may cause
readers, no responsibility for any such changes can be
accepted by either the author or the publishers.

The paper used to print this book comes from
sustainable resources.

CONTENTS

FAST AND FURIOUS   47902   4

ON THE ROAD   662118   SCH
                          J629.22   6

SPORTS CAR PARTS   16

SUPERCARS   28

CLASSIC SPORTS CARS   32

RACING SPORTS CARS   38

MAKERS AND DESIGNERS   48

DESIGNING A SUPERCAR   56

SPORTS CAR FACTS   58

FIND OUT FOR YOURSELF   60

GLOSSARY   62

INDEX   64

Any words appearing in the text in bold, **like this**, are explained in the Glossary. You can also look out for them in the Up To Speed box at the bottom of each page.

FAST AND FURIOUS

SPORTS CAR TERMS

Some sidebars like this one contain details of sports cars. This is what some of the words in the sidebars mean.

bhp: short for **brake horse power**. Engine power is measured in bhp

km/h: short for kilometres per hour

mph: short for miles per hour

rpm: short for **revolutions** per minute

The driver turns a key and puts the car into gear. He presses his foot onto the **accelerator** and the engine roars into life. The tyres screech on the **tarmac** and the car leaps forward. The driver is thrown back into the seat as the car speeds away. Seconds later the car is hurtling along at terrifying speed. This is no ordinary car! It is a sports car. It is sleek and powerful. It was built for having fun!

FAMOUS NAMES

There are plenty of famous sports car makers, and plenty of famous sports cars. Have you heard of Ferrari, Jaguar, Lamborghini and Audi? They are all sports car makers. What about the Viper, the Corvette, the Testarossa and the DB9? These are all famous sports cars.

accelerator   foot pedal used to make a car's engine produce more or less power

ASTON MARTIN DB9

- Date production started: 2003
- **Chassis** (pronounced, 'shass-ee'), the structure of a car: **aluminium** frame
- Engine position: front (see pages 14–15)
- Engine type: 6.0-litre V12
- Power: 450 bhp
- **Acceleration**: 0–60 mph (96 km/h) in 4.7 seconds
- Top speed: 186 mph (298 km/h)

ROAD AND TRACK

You often see beautiful sports cars whizzing by on the streets. This is where most lucky owners drive their cars. But to see sports cars performing at their best you have to go to a race track. Here you can watch expert racing drivers thundering around corners at incredible speeds.

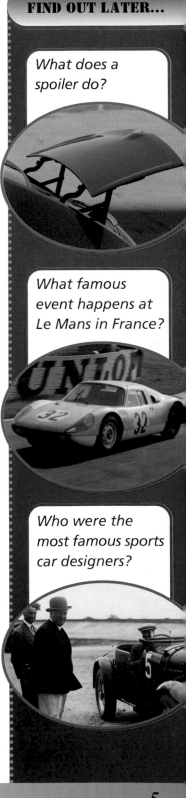

What does a spoiler do?

What famous event happens at Le Mans in France?

Who were the most famous sports car designers?

---

aluminium a strong, lightweight material
tarmac hard, smooth road covering

ON THE ROAD

What is a sports car? There's no exact answer to this question. But it is different from an ordinary family car. A sports car is normally quite small. It is low slung. That means it is lower than a normal car. The biggest difference between a sports car and a family car is performance. Performance is how quickly a car can accelerate, and how fast it can go. Sports cars have great performance. A sports car must also handle well. That means it must corner at high speed without spinning out of control.

PERFORMANCE FIGURES

Sports car **enthusiasts** like to compare the performance of different cars. Performance is measured by **acceleration** and top speed. Acceleration can be measured by the time it takes the car to reach 60 mph (96 km/h) from standing still.

The 165-mph (265 km/h) Dodge Viper is one of the USA's best sports cars.

chassis   framework that supports a car's body

FUN TO DRIVE

People can drive sports cars on the public roads. However, there are speed limits for safety on public roads, so sports car owners cannot drive their machines at top speed. They have to go to a race track instead.

People still love driving sports cars on the roads. They enjoy feeling the power from the engine as the car accelerates. They love the feeling of speed, especially in an open sports car. And they enjoy the thrill of driving round corners at high speed.

BMW Z8

- Date production started: 2000
- Where made: Germany
- **Chassis**: tubular **aluminium**
- Engine position: front (see pages 14–15)
- Engine type: 5.0-litre V8
- Power: 394 bhp
- Acceleration: 0–60 mph (96 km/h) in 4.7 seconds
- Top speed: 155 mph (249 km/h)

enthusiast   person who really enjoys a particular hobby

Most sports cars have only two seats, one for the driver and one for a passenger. Sometimes there is a small, cramped space for another passenger behind. There's not much room for luggage. After all, sports cars are for fun!

SPORTY LOOKS

There are lots of differences between a sports car and an ordinary four-seater family car. The difference that is easiest to see is the shape. A sports car has a smoother, lower body than a family car. This smooth shape lets the car move easily through the air. A sports car is low to the ground to keep its centre of gravity low. Its centre of gravity is the point around which it balances. A low centre of gravity makes a sports car very stable. It lets the car go round corners fast without tipping over.

TECH TALK

Features of a sports car
• Smooth body
• Low, wide shape
• Lightweight parts
• Powerful engine

LIGHT AND POWERFUL

Sports cars can pull away quickly from a standing start. They speed up quickly, too. They leave family cars standing still. We say that sports cars have good **acceleration**. Acceleration depends on weight and power. The lighter the car and the more powerful its engine, the better its acceleration will be. Sports cars are lightweight and have powerful engines. A powerful engine also gives the car a good top speed.

TWO DOORS

Most sports cars have two doors, one on each side. A few have no doors at all — the driver has to climb in the top. Some sports cars feature doors called 'scissor' doors. They open upwards instead of outwards.

This front-on view of a Dodge Viper shows its low, sleek shape.

RENAULT CLIO SPORT

- Date production started: 1998
- Where made: France
- **Chassis: unitary**
- Engine position: front (see pages 14–15)
- Engine type: 3.0-litre V6
- Power: 230 bhp
- **Acceleration:** 0–60 mph (96 km/h) in 6.7 seconds
- Top speed: 145 mph (233 km/h)

SPORTS CAR STYLES

All sports cars are sleek, low machines. But that's only half the story. They come in different styles and each style has its own name. A **roadster** is a two-seater sports car with no roof. There is just a windscreen to protect the passengers from the wind and rain. This style of car is sometimes called a spyder. This was the Italian name given to a roadster in the early 1900s. A **coupé** (pronounced, 'coo-pay') is a sports car with a body that curves gently from the roof to the rear. This style of car is often known as a **grand tourer**, or **GT**.

alloy wheels   wheels made from lightweight alloy metal

CONVERTIBLES

Many sports cars are also **convertibles**. A convertible has a roof that the driver can put on when it is cold or rainy, or take off when it is dry and sunny. Convertibles have either soft tops or hard tops. Soft tops are made of fabric on a metal frame. Hard tops are made of metal or plastic. Tops can be removed completely or can fold down into a space in the boot. Cars with folding roofs are often called **drop-tops**. Sports cars that are not convertible, especially coupés, are often called **fixed-heads**.

SPORTS SALOON

A few sports cars are sporty versions of ordinary saloon cars. A saloon car has four seats, a fixed roof, and luggage space in the boot. Sports saloons have more powerful engines than ordinary saloons, and other features such as spoilers and **alloy wheels**.

The Mazda RX-8 is a coupé or fixed-head sports car.

unitary chassis   framework that includes a car's side and roof panels, floor and engine compartment

Inside a Honda Civic Type-R. The speedometer and rev counter are big and clear.

x1000

REV COUNTER RED LINE

The speed of an engine is measured in **revolutions** per minute (rpm). A red line on the rev counter shows the driver the maximum speed that the engine can turn without being damaged.

SPORTING INTERIORS

The outside of a sports car is different to the outside of an ordinary family car. But how is the inside of a sports car different to the inside of an ordinary car? What are the dashboard, seats and controls like? Some very expensive sports cars are very luxurious. There are expensive materials such as leather and polished wood. Other sports cars are very simple inside. This is to keep the car's weight down for maximum performance. Even some incredibly expensive cars have very simple cabins.

crankshaft   part of an engine that turns and is connected to the transmission

Most sports cars have manual **transmission**. That means the driver changes gear to go faster or slower by moving a gear stick. A few sports cars have semi-automatic transmission. The driver changes gear by pulling on small paddles on the steering wheel.

INSTRUMENTS

A sports car needs the same instruments as any other car. But the most important are the **speedometer** and **rev counter**. The speedometer shows the car's speed, and the rev counter shows how quickly the engine's **crankshaft** is turning.

SEATS AND BELTS

As a sports car accelerates, brakes and speeds round corners, the driver and passenger are thrown about. Sports car seats have side supports to stop people in them from sliding backwards, forwards or sideways. They are called bucket seats. Sports cars often have four-point seat belts, which hold the occupants in their seats more firmly than normal three-point belts.

revolution   one complete turn
transmission   machinery that connects a car's engine to its wheels

ENGINE POSITIONS

The engine of a sports car gives it its speedy performance. Together with the **transmission**, the engine makes up the heaviest part of a car. The position of this weight in the car is important for good handling.

FRONT AND REAR

In most ordinary cars the engine is at the front. It is ahead of the driver. This means that most of the weight of the engine is on the front wheels. Most sports cars also have the engine at the front. Front-engined sports cars often have a long bonnet. A few sports cars have the engine behind the rear wheels. The back of a rear-engined car tends to swing out on corners if the driver is not very careful. This puts the car into a spin.

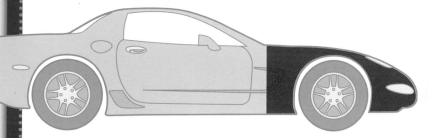

DRIVING WHEELS

The driving wheels are the wheels that the engine turns round. Sports cars either have **rear-wheel drive**, **front-wheel drive** or **four-wheel drive**. Most sports cars have rear-wheel drive. This helps to stop the wheels spinning because the car leans back onto the rear wheels as the car accelerates, pressing them onto the road. This Citroën is a four-wheel drive rally car.

The orange highlight shows the engine position in a front-engined car (above), a mid-engined car (top right) and a rear-engined car (bottom right).

front-wheel drive   vehicle that has its front wheels turned directly by the engine

MID-ENGINES

Some sports cars have mid-engines. That means that the engine is behind the driver but in front of the rear wheels. It is where the back seats would be in a normal family car. The weight of the engine is shared between the front and back wheels. A mid-engined car turns into corners better than a front-engined car.

PAGANI ZONDA

- Date production started: 1999
- Where made: Italy
- **Chassis: monocoque**
- Engine position: mid-engined
- Engine type: 6.0-litre V12
- Power: 388 bhp
- **Acceleration:** 0–60 mph (96 km/h) in 4.5 seconds
- Top speed: 200 mph (322 km/h)

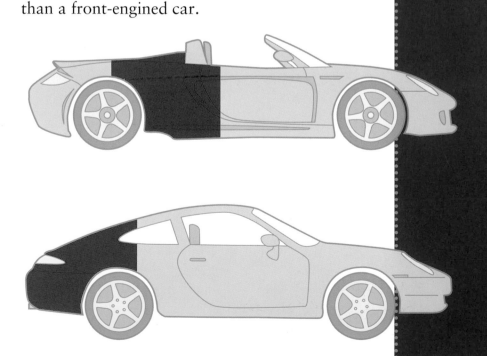

monocoque   single-piece chassis
rear-wheel drive   vehicle that has its rear wheels turned directly by the engine

SPORTS CAR PARTS

Sports cars must have quick **acceleration**, top speeds and stable handling. This is not easy for **manufacturers** to achieve. They use special car bodies, special engines and many other special parts for their cars. You can't build a sports car from ordinary car parts!

SPOILERS AND WINGS

Sports cars often have a piece like a shelf at the rear. This is called a spoiler. It reduces drag. Some sports cars have a wing instead of a spoiler. At high speed it presses the car's wheels onto the road for better grip.

SMOOTH BODIES

Sports car bodies are not made in sleek shapes just to look good. A smooth, curved shape is important for performance, too. It is all to do with **aerodynamics**.

Air flowing smoothly over a sports-car body in a wind tunnel.

aerodynamics   science of how air flows around moving objects

PUSHING THE AIR ASIDE

As a car speeds along it must push the air in front
of it aside. The air causes a force on the front of the
car that tries to slow the car down. The force is
called air resistance or **drag**. The faster a car goes,
the bigger the drag gets. Eventually drag stops a car
going any faster. Air flows more easily around a
smooth car than a vehicle with a bulky shape. The
smooth car has less drag on it. So it can go faster.

REDUCING DRAG

Any part of a car that sticks out into the air
creates drag. The only bits that stick out from a
very fast sports car are the wing
mirrors. These are specially designed
to make as little drag as possible.
Sports cars also have **faired-in**
headlamps or pop-up headlamps.

The bottom of a
sports car is very
close to the
ground. This helps
to reduce drag
and sucks the car
down onto the
road. The front air
deflector pushes
air into the engine
cooling ducts and
around the car's
sides.

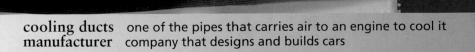

SPORTS CHASSIS

The main part of a car is its **chassis**. All the other parts of a car attach to the chassis. A chassis must be strong for safety and for handling. Ordinary family cars have a one-piece chassis made from steel. It includes side and roof panels, a floor and engine compartment. This is called a **unitary chassis**.

Steel is a heavy material. For good **acceleration** and braking a sports car needs to be lightweight. A steel unitary chassis would slow its performance. Sports cars are made lightweight by using special materials and structures.

SPECIAL MATERIALS

Many sports cars have a unitary body shell made from **aluminium**. Doors and bonnets are made from aluminium, too. Aluminium is lighter than steel, but it is more expensive. Body panels are often made from other tough lightweight materials, such as plastic, **carbon fibre** and **kevlar**.

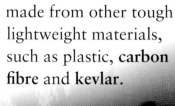

MONOCOQUES

A **monocoque** (pronounced, 'mon-o-cock') is another type of chassis. A monocoque is a super-strong internal box (see blue area in diagram below) that surrounds the driver and passenger. All the other parts of the car are attached to it. This design is very strong and incredibly light.

carbon fibre   very hard, strong, light material

PE51 XBV

TVR CERBERA

- Date production started: 1995
- Where made: UK
- Chassis: tubular
- Engine position: front
- Engine type: 4.2-litre V8
- Power: 350 bhp
- **Acceleration**: 0–60 mph (96 km/h) in 4.0 seconds
- Top speed: 185 mph (297 km/h)

INTERNAL FRAMES

Very light, very fast sports cars do not normally have unitary bodies. Instead they have a lightweight internal frame. Thin body panels are attached to it. The frame gives the car strength and supports the engine and other parts. The body panels give it style and make it **aerodynamic**. Some sports cars have a space frame. This is made from steel or aluminium tubes, a bit like a bicycle frame.

The Noble M12 is built around a steel space-frame chassis.

kevlar very strong type of fibre

Four strokes
These are the strokes of a four-stroke engine.

1. Intake stroke
Piston moves out of the cylinder. Air and fuel mixture goes into the cylinder.

2. Compression stroke
Piston moves into the cylinder. Air and fuel is squashed into the top of the cylinder.

3. Power stroke
Fuel and air explodes. Piston is pushed out of the cylinder.

4. Exhaust stroke
Piston moves into the cylinder. Waste gases are pushed out of the cylinder.

POWERFUL ENGINES

A sports car engine is very similar to the engine of a normal family car. It is called an **internal combustion** engine and looks like a big block of metal. Inside are spaces called **cylinders**. They are the shape of tin cans. Inside each cylinder is a piston. The **piston** fits tightly into the cylinder, but it can slide in and out. The engine's power comes from tiny explosions that push the pistons outwards. The moving pistons make a part called a **crankshaft** turn. The crankshaft drives the car's wheels and the car speeds off.

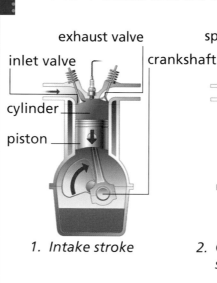

exhaust valve   spark plug

inlet valve   crankshaft

cylinder

piston

1. Intake stroke

2. Compression stroke

3. Power stroke

4. Exhaust stroke

internal combustion   what happens when fuel burns inside the engine

FOUR-STROKE CYCLE

The pistons in an engine keep going out then in, out then in. Each movement in or out is called a stroke. Every piston does a pattern of four strokes (see sidebar on page 20). Each pattern is called a cycle. During each cycle fuel is burned in the cylinder to make an explosion. Waste gases made by the explosion are pushed out, making the cylinder ready for the next cycle. The fuel for most sports car engines is petrol. The petrol is turned into tiny droplets and mixed with air before it goes into the cylinder. The explosion is set off by a tiny spark made by a **spark plug**.

CYLINDERS AND VALVES

Each cylinder in an engine has holes in the top that let fuel and air in and let exhaust gases out. Each hole has a **valve** that opens and closes the hole. Rotating rods called **cam shafts** make the valves open and close.

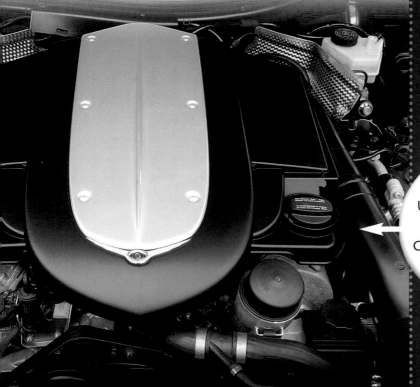

Under the bonnet of the Chrysler Crossfire sports car.

---

spark plug   device that makes a spark so that fuel explodes in an engine
valve   allows movement of a fluid in one direction only

ENGINE STATISTICS

The **capacity** of an engine is the space inside its **cylinders**. The bigger the capacity of an engine the more powerful it is. Capacity is measured in cubic centimetres (cc) or litres. Normal family cars have engines with capacities from about 1000 cc (1 litre) to about 2000 cc. Many sports car engines have capacities of more than 3000 cc. Some engines are as big as 6000 cc. An engine's power is measured in **brake horse power** (bhp). A normal car engine produces between 50 and 120 bhp. Small sports car engines produce more than 150 bhp. Big ones produce more than 500 bhp.

PORSCHE V10

This engine powers the Porsche Carrera GT
• Type: V10
• Capacity: 5.7 litres
• Maximum revs: over 8000 rpm
• **Valves**: four per cylinder
• Power: 603 bhp
• **Transmission**: six speed manual

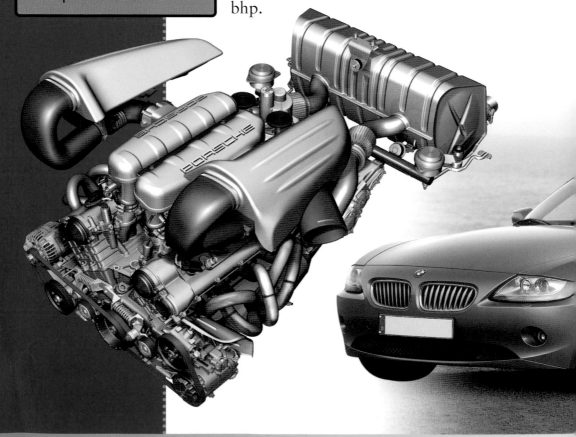

brake horse power (bhp)   a measurement of engine power

V6

Flat 12

Straight 4

ENGINE ARRANGEMENTS

Normal car engines have only four cylinders. They are arranged in a straight line. This is called a straight-four engine. Sports car engines have six, eight, ten or even twelve cylinders. In these engines the cylinders are in two rows. Half the cylinders are in one side of the engine and half in the other side. The cylinders are tilted outwards to make a V shape. This sort of engine is called a V6, a V8, a V10 or a V12. In a few engines the two rows of cylinders are on their sides, opposite each other. This is called a flat engine.

HIGH REVS

Each time a **piston** does its power stroke it produces power for the car's wheels. The more often pistons do power strokes, the more power an engine produces. Normal car engines can rev up to about 6000 rpm. Sports engines can rev up to about 8000 rpm. A normal engine would break apart at this rate!

The BMW Z4 has a 3-litre, straight-6 engine arrangement.

SUPERCHARGED

In most car engines, the **pistons** suck air and fuel into the **cylinders** on the intake stroke. Sports-car engines often have **superchargers** or **turbochargers**. These are pumps that force air and fuel into the cylinders. This lets the engine burn more fuel on each stroke, so it is more powerful. A supercharger pump is worked by the engine. A turbocharger pump is worked by the exhaust gases flowing out of the engine.

EXHAUSTS AND SILENCERS

High capacity, high-revving sports car engines produce lots of exhaust gases. They often have twin exhausts, with twin catalytic converters – these take poisonous gases out of the exhaust gases. Silencer boxes reduce the noise of the exhaust gases roaring from the engine.

The twin exhaust pipes at the rear of a TVR T440R.

clutch   device that is used to change gear

TRANSMISSIONS

A car's **transmission** connects its engine to its wheels. The transmission's gears allow the engine to turn the wheels at different speeds. Low gears are for starting off and high gears for high-speed driving. Transmissions can be manual, automatic and semi-automatic. In a manual transmission the driver changes gear with a gear lever and **clutch** pedal. An automatic transmission changes gear by itself as the car speeds up and slows down.

◀ ◀ ◀ ◀ ◀ ◀ ◀ ◀ ◀ ◀ ◀

Find out more about semi-automatic transmission on page 13.

TOYOTA SUPRA

- Date production started: 1993
- Where made: Japan
- **Chassis: unitary**
- Engine position: front
- Engine type: 3.0-litre twin turbo straight 6
- Power: 326 bhp
- **Acceleration**: 0–60 mph (96 km/h) in 5.1 seconds
- Top speed: 155 mph (249 km/h)

---

supercharger device that blows air into an engine, driven by the engine
turbocharger device that blows air into an engine, driven by exhaust gases

WHEELS

Sports cars have special wheels to increase their performance. Sports wheels are made from lightweight metals called **alloys**. They are lighter than the solid steel wheels on ordinary cars. Tyres are the only parts of a car that touch the road. Sports cars need to grip the road well for performance and safety. Grip comes from the **friction** between the tyres and the road surface. Sports cars tyres are wider than ordinary tyres. Wide tyres have more rubber in contact with the road, giving the extra grip that sports cars need. Grooves in the tyres, called tread, squeeze water from under the tyres.

SUSPENSIONS

Sports cars have stiff **suspensions** to stop them rolling from side to side on bumpy roads and sharp bends. Many sports cars have a special suspension called a double-wishbone suspension. It keeps the tyres flat on the road all the time.

   air scoop   one of the holes in a car body that funnels air to cool the brakes

An alloy sports car wheel fitted with a low-profile sports tyre.

SPEEDING UP

As a sports car speeds up, the wide tyres push back on the road. This pushes the car forwards. As the car brakes, the wide tyres push forwards on the road, slowing it quickly. As the car zips round a corner, the tyres push sideways, stopping the car from sliding.

SLOWING DOWN

Sports cars need strong brakes for slowing quickly from high speed. Each wheel has a disc attached to it. When the driver presses the brake pedal, brake pads press hard on the discs. Friction between the pads and discs slows the car. Bigger sports cars often have two sets of pads on each disc for extra stopping power.

COOLING BRAKES

Friction between brake pads and discs makes lots of heat. Sports car brakes can get very hot. The discs and pads are made from special materials that do not melt. **Air scoops** make air flow over the brakes, helping to cool them.

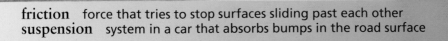

friction   force that tries to stop surfaces sliding past each other
suspension   system in a car that absorbs bumps in the road surface

SUPERCARS

Some sports cars are very special. They have amazing **acceleration** and surprising top speeds. These are the **supercars**. They are the kings of the sports car world. They also have incredible prices. They are so expensive that only top sports stars, pop stars and wealthy business people can afford to buy them.

PEAK PERFORMANCE

Supercars are the ultimate road-going cars. Top supercars accelerate as quickly as **Formula One** racing cars and easily match their top speeds. From a standing start, a supercar reaches 60 mph (96 km/h) in around 4 seconds. A few seconds later it can be travelling at more than 200 mph (320 km/h). For performance like this a supercar needs an engine that produces more than 500 bhp. The car needs to be made of lightweight materials.

SUPERCAR BUILDERS

Supercars are normally designed to be driven on the road. Special versions of them are built for the race track. Other supercars are road-going versions of racing cars. Supercar manufacturers like to hold the title of World's Fastest **Production Car**. In 2003 this was held by the McLaren F1, at 240 mph (386 km/h). Famous supercar makers include Jaguar, Ferrari and Lamborghini.

MERCEDES McLAREN SLR

- Date production started: 2004
- Where made: Germany
- **Chassis: carbon-fibre monocoque**
- Engine position: front
- Engine type: 5.5 litre **supercharged** V8
- Power: 626 bhp
- Acceleration: 0–60 mph (96 km/h) in 3.8 seconds
- Top speed: 208 mph (335 km/h)

The body panels and doors of the Mercedes SLR are made from lightweight **aluminium.**

RACING TECHNOLOGY

The engineers who design racing cars are always developing new ways to make their cars faster, easier to drive and safer. **Supercar** makers often build racing cars, too. They use technology from their racing cars in their supercars. Some supercars are really racing cars with alterations to make them 'street legal'. They have a lightweight racing-car **chassis**, high-power racing engines, and racing-car controls.

McLAREN F1

The McLaren F1 was the World's Fastest **Production Car** for over ten years. It costs more than half a million pounds to buy one. The F1 was based on McLaren's successful Formula One racing car.

McLAREN F1

- Date production started: 1993
- Where made: UK
- Chassis: carbon-fibre monocoque
- Engine position: mid-engined
- Engine type: 6.0-litre V12
- Power: 627 bhp
- **Acceleration**: 0–60 mph (96 km/h) in 3.2 seconds
- Top speed: 240 mph (386 km/h)

carbon fibre   very hard, strong, light material

FORMULA ONE ROAD CAR

The Ferrari F50 supercar was designed and built to celebrate the 50th birthday of the Ferrari company. The car was based on Ferrari's **Formula One** racing car used in the 1990 season. Underneath the bright red body is a super-strong, **carbon-fibre, monocoque** chassis. Bolted to the back of the monocoque is a 4.7-litre V12 engine. It is a bigger version of the engine from the racing car. The F50 has electronically controlled **suspension** that adjusts to how rough the road is.

The F50 is not a luxury supercar. The engine is very noisy and the cockpit is quite bare. But this makes drivers feel they are sitting in a road-going racer!

Q&A

Q: How many Ferrari F50 cars were built?

A: Only 349.

The Ferrari F50's body was designed by Pininfarina.

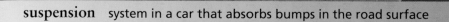

F50 CON

MARANELLO SALES LTD

---

suspension   system in a car that absorbs bumps in the road surface

CLASSIC SPORTS CARS

The very first motor car was built by German engineer Karl Benz in 1885. It looked like a horse-drawn carriage with an engine bolted on the back. In fact, that is exactly what it was. Engine power was just one horsepower. Top speed was just 9 mph (14 km/h). Benz's car was an amazing machine at the time, but it was hardly a sports car! Motor engineers quickly designed more powerful engines, giving cars better top speeds. Soon drivers became interested in going fast. They also started racing against each other.

EARLY AERODYNAMICS

In the 1920s racing-car makers began designing **aerodynamic** bodies to make their cars faster. Sports car **manufacturers** copied the idea. They designed the first **coupés**. This style of car became known as the **grand tourer** or GT.

◄◄◄◄◄◄◄◄◄◄
Find out more about the GT on page 10.

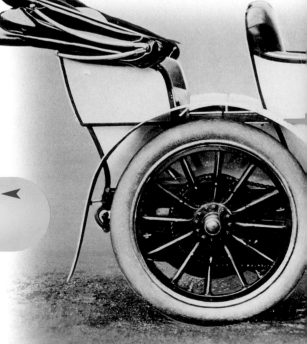

coupé   sports car with a body that curves gently from the roof to the rear

THE FIRST SPORTS CAR

Most car historians think that the first proper sports car was the Mercedes 35 hp. This car was built in 1901 by the Daimler company in Germany. The '35 hp' part of the name stood for 35 horse power. This was the power of the engine. The car was called Mercedes after the daughter of one of Daimler's salesmen. The Mercedes 35 hp had many new technical ideas, including a lightweight **chassis** and mechanical engine **valves**. It outperformed other cars of the time and won many races. Top speed was more than 60 mph (96 km/h).

A **supercharger** makes an engine more powerful. The supercharger was invented in the 1920s for racing cars. It soon appeared on road-going cars too. This Bugatti type 55 was one of the first road cars to have a supercharger.

◀◀◀◀◀◀◀◀◀◀◀◀
Find out how a supercharger works on page 24.

The Mercedes 35-hp was designed by the famous German engineer Wilhelm Maybach.

FASTER AND FASTER

Dozens of companies in Europe and the USA were building sports cars when World War Two began in 1939. By then the best sports cars could manage top speeds of more than 100 mph (160 km/h).

FIRST TO 120 MPH

The Jaguar XK120 was shown to the public for the first time at the 1948 London Motor Show. The '120' part of its name stood for 120 mph (193 km/h). The XK120 was the first **production car** that could reach that speed. The engine was so good that it was still being put into new Jaguars in the 1990s. The XK120 was very popular in the USA, where there were few sports cars.

A Jaguar XK120 taking part in a race in the 1950s.

production car   car built in large numbers for general sale

ITALIAN AND AMERICAN FIRSTS

One of Ferrari's first sports cars was also built in 1948. It was the Ferrari 166 Inter, designed by Enzo Ferrari. Ferrari only made the **chassis** and engine. Customers had to buy their own bodywork. Top speed for the 166 was 105 mph (169 km/h). Until the 1950s most sports cars bought by Americans were made in Europe. Then the USA **manufacturer** General Motors designed the famous Chevrolet Corvette. The original straight-6 engine was replaced by a more powerful V8, which improved its top speed to 120 mph (193 km/h).

007'S ASTON MARTIN

Aston Martin is a famous British sports car maker. Its Aston Martin DB5 **coupé** (pictured above) was made famous in 1964 by the James Bond film Goldfinger. Bond's DB5 also had machine guns and an ejector seat.

CHEVROLET CORVETTE

- Date production started: 1953
- Where made: USA
- Chassis: box section
- Engine position: front
- Engine type: 3.8-litre straight 6
- Power: 150 bhp
- **Acceleration**: 0–60 mph (96 km/h) in 11.2 seconds
- Top speed: 105 mph (169 km/h)

AGE OF THE SUPERCARS

In the 1960s a new type of sports car appeared on the roads. It was the **supercar**. These extraordinary cars featured a mixture of enormous power, beautiful design and huge price tags. The Italian company Lamborghini was one of the first supercar **manufacturers**. Its first car was built in 1966. It was called the Miura. It had a top speed of 171 mph (275 km/h). A few years later Lamborghini replaced the Miura with a new model, the Countach. Its 3.9-litre V12 engine gave it a top speed of 175 mph (282 km/h). Both cars were mid-engined.

LAMBORGHINI COUNTACH

- Date production started: 1971
- Where made: Italy
- **Chassis**: tubular steel
- Engine position: mid-engined
- Engine type: 3.9-litre V12
- Power: 375 bhp
- **Acceleration**: 0–60 mph (96 km/h) in 5.7 seconds
- Top speed: 175 mph (282 km/h)

NASCAR   short for National Association for Stock Car Auto Racing

OLD AND NEW STYLES

Most modern sports cars have a sleek look. They have smooth, rounded, **aerodynamic** bodies. They are definitely machines of the twenty-first century. But many sports-car **enthusiasts** love the look of the two-seater sports cars of the 1920s and 1930s. Real classic cars are hard to find and expensive to buy and repair. So a few manufacturers build new sports cars in the old style. They have narrow bodies, arches over the wheels and small windscreens. Some examples are the Morgan 8 and the Caterham 7, both made in the UK. These cars might look old, but underneath they are modern sports machines.

The Morgan Aero 8. Classic style with modern technology.

ROAD RUNNER

The extraordinary Plymouth Road Runner Superbird was named after the Road Runner cartoon character. It was designed for the road and for racing in American **NASCAR** races. On the track it could reach 190 mph (306 km/h).

Y415 CGK

RACING SPORTS CARS

When you think of a racing car, you probably think of a purpose-built racer such as a **Formula One** car or American **Indy Car**. But most motor races are between sports cars like the ones you see on the public roads.

LACK OF LUXURY

Racing sports cars are not built for comfort! The car is stripped of all its luxury fittings for the race track. It makes the car lighter. Only the most important controls and instruments are left.

RACING MODIFICATIONS

Sports cars designed for the public roads are **modified** for the track. The modifications improve the car's performance, allowing it to speed up faster, brake more quickly and corner faster. Wings and skirts are **aerodynamic** modifications. They help to press the car onto the road for better grip on corners. Racing tyres made from soft rubber also make the car grip better. Stronger brakes allow drivers to brake later as they approach corners.

The racing version of the Peugeot 307 with spoiler and **alloy wheels**.

capacity   total space inside all the cylinders of a car engine
Indy Car   type of racing in the USA similar to Formula One

ENGINE TUNING

Racing cars have more powerful engines than road-going sports cars. Sometimes the engine has a bigger **capacity**. It is also race **tuned**, which means adjustments are made to get the most power possible from the engine. The **valve** timings are adjusted. That means the engine's valves open and close at exactly the right time for fuel and air to get into the cylinders and for exhaust gases to get out. The air inlets and exhausts are bigger. This lets more fuel in and more exhaust gases out.

MERCEDES BENZ CLK-GTR

- Date production started: 1998
- Where made: Germany
- **Chassis: carbon-fibre monocoque**
- Engine position: mid-engined
- Engine type: 6.8-litre V12
- Power: 612 bhp
- **Acceleration**: 0–60 mph (96 km/h) in 3.8 seconds
- Top speed: 199 mph (320 km/h)

The road-going **convertible** version of the Peugeot 307.

tuned   adjusted to give maximum power

ONE-MODEL RACE

A one-model race is a race for just one model of sports car. These races are for sports car owners who want to try out their driving skills on the race track.

TRACK RACING

Most sports car races are held on race tracks. There are many different race-track competitions. Some competitions are single races for local drivers. The drivers own the cars and service them themselves. Some competitions are world **championships** which are made up of many races on different race tracks. The cars are built by sports car **manufacturers** and driven by **professional** drivers.

RACING CLASSES

Sports cars are divided into different classes for racing. This means that cars with similar performance race against each other. Some competitions are reserved for road-going sports cars and some are for purpose-built racing cars which are built just for racing.

Drivers warm up their tyres on a practice lap before the big race.

TOP RACES

The World **GT** Car Championship is for road-going sports cars. The Sportscar Championship is for purpose-built racing sports cars. In the USA the top sports car championship is **NASCAR**. Years ago NASCAR cars were **production cars** **modified** for the race track. Now they are built just for racing.

A NASCAR pit stop. The team are changing tyres and refuelling.

RULES

Each competition has it own strict rules. Technical rules tell the engineers exactly what features the cars are allowed to have. For example, they specify the maximum or minimum size of the car's body, the engine size and tyre sizes.

PRODUCTION CAR RULES

There is a special rule for production sports car racing. A certain number of each car model must be made for use on the road before that model can enter a race.

professional   person who gets paid for driving a car

RACING AT LE MANS

The Le Mans 24-Hour Race is one of the world's most famous sports car races. It is not only a race, but also a gruelling test of endurance for both cars and drivers. The car that travels furthest in 24 hours is the winner. The race is held every year near Le Mans in France.

THE COURSE

The Le Mans course is 13.6 km (8.5 miles) long. It is made up of the Sarthe motor-racing circuit and some lengths of public roads.

The most famous part of the circuit is the Mulsanne straight, which is 5.7 km (3.5 miles) long. By 1989 cars were whizzing down the straight at more than 250 mph (400 km/h). After that, **chicanes** were added to slow the cars for safety.

LE MANS TYPES

Two types of cars can enter Le Mans. The first type is **GT** sports cars. These must be racing models of road-going **production cars,** such as the Porsche 911 GT and the Ferrari 360 Modena. The second type is prototype cars. These are purpose-built single-seater racing sports cars. They are built and raced by major **manufacturers** such as Audi and BMW. A prototype car almost always wins the race because prototypes have better performance than road-going cars.

This is the road-going version of the Dodge Viper GTS-R that races at Le Mans.

DODGE VIPER GTS-R

- Date production started: 2000
- Where made: USA
- **Chassis**: tubular
- Engine position: front
- Engine type: 8-litre V10
- Power: 500 bhp
- **Acceleration**: 0–60 mph (96 km/h) in 5.3 seconds
- Top speed: 172 mph (277 km/h)

RALLY RACING

Sports cars also race in **rallies**. A rally is a long-distance race along public roads, rough tracks and across country. Rally cars hurtle over **tarmac**, dusty gravel, mud and ice at speeds of up to 125 mph (200 km/h). The top race in rallying is the World Rally **Championship**. Teams take part in 14 rallies around the world. Each rally lasts for three days and is made up of about twenty sections called stages. The cars drive over the stages one after the other. The times for each stage are added together and the car with the quickest time wins.

co-driver   in rallying, a person who gives the driver information about the road ahead

RALLY CAR FEATURES

Rally cars must be extremely tough to stay in one piece on the bumpy roads. World rally cars are **modified** production sports cars. But only the shape of the car is left!

A world rally car costs about half a million pounds to make. It has a super-strong **chassis** and a **roll cage** to protect the driver and **co-driver**. Its 2-litre **turbocharged** engine produces 300 bhp. The gears are semi-automatic and change up or down in less than a tenth of a second. After each stage, mechanics are allowed just 20 minutes to repair the cars.

The service area at the 2003 Rally of Catalonia.

SUBARU IMPREZA WRX

- Date production started: 1993
- Where made: Japan
- Chassis: **unitary**
- Engine position: front
- Engine type: 2-litre flat 4
- Power: 280 bhp
- **Acceleration**: 0–60 mph (96 km/h) in 4.7 seconds
- Top speed: 150 mph (241 km/h)

DRIVING A SPORTS CAR

Driving a sports car at high speed is very different to driving an ordinary family car around town. A sports car driver needs quick reactions. This means they can recover from skids or swerves and overtake and avoid other cars. Races are often won by the driver who takes the track's corners at the highest speed possible. Slowing too much for a corner wastes time. But if a driver takes a corner too fast the tyres cannot grip the road and the car spins off the track.

SAFETY FIRST

Even the best race drivers sometimes crash in their sports cars. But modern sports cars are very safe. They feature strong **roll cages** and seat belts. The driver also wears a crash helmet and fireproof overalls.

MAKING ADJUSTMENTS

Racing drivers also have to understand how their cars work. Cars often oversteer or understeer on corners. That means they turn too much or not enough. Drivers must understand why this happens. They ask the team's mechanics to make adjustments to the car's wings and **suspension** to put the problem right.

RALLY DRIVERS

Rally drivers have to concentrate hard to drive flat-out on narrow, bumpy, slippery roads. The **co-driver** tells the driver what bends, bumps and other obstacles are coming up on the road.

THE RACING LINE

Drivers try to learn the fastest way around a race track before racing for real. They work out where to start turning to take each corner and what line to take through the corner. Drivers call this the racing line.

Rally cars often get airborne on humps and bumps.

MAKERS AND DESIGNERS

Motor **manufacturers** such as Ferrari, Audi and Jaguar have become famous for their sports cars. People expect these cars to have great looks as well as great performance, so it is important to have a good **stylist** to design the cars. A few sports car stylists have become as famous as the cars they designed.

A BUGATTI REVIVAL

Volkswagen took over the Bugatti name in 1998. They built a Bugatti **supercar** called the Veyron in 2004. It is the fastest **production car** ever.

▶▶▶▶▶▶▶▶▶▶

Find out more about the Veyron on page 57.

BUGATTI

Bugatti is one of the most famous names in sports car history. Bugatti's best cars were made in the 1920s and 1930s. They won many races on the track, including Le Mans in the 1930s. The Bugatti company was started in 1910 by Italian motor designer Ettore Bugatti.

Ettore Bugatti (standing, in hat) and Jean Bugatti (in car) in 1939.

BUGATTI'S CARS

Ettore Bugatti designed the Type 35 Bugatti in 1924. Many **enthusiasts** think this two-seater is the most beautiful sports car ever made. Ettore's eldest son was Jean Bugatti. Jean was a great engineer and a talented stylist. He designed the streamlined Bugatti cars of the 1930s, such as the Type 57 **coupé**. Jean was killed in 1939 testing one of his own cars. Ettore died in 1947 and the company stopped making cars.

THE FAMOUS BUGATTI RADIATOR

Every sports car maker has its own symbol that appears on every car. Every Bugatti had a **radiator** shaped like an upside-down horseshoe (see blue Bugatti on page 48). At the top is a red badge with the famous Bugatti name.

A Bugatti at a vintage car rally event.

ITALIAN STYLE

Italy was the home of the greatest sports car **stylists**. They designed cars for famous **manufacturers** in Italy and in other countries too. Pininfarina is a company that is famous for its car design. It was started by Giovan (pronounced, 'jo-van') Battista Farina (left). He had nine older brothers and was known as 'Pinin'. That means 'little boy' in Italian. Farina was born in 1895 and started his career at his brother's car-making company. He started Pininfarina in 1930. The company designed cars for Lancia and Fiat. Its most famous designs were for Ferrari, such as the Ferrari Daytona, Ferrari F-40 and Ferrari Enzo.

The Dino of the 1960s, one of Pininfarina's designs for Fiat.

GHIA

The word 'Ghia' appears on many modern Ford cars. It means that the car has special extras such as **alloy** **wheels** and electric windows. Ghia was an Italian company named after designer Giacinto Ghia. It built sports car bodies for Alfa Romeo, Maserati and Porsche.

alloy wheels   wheels made from lightweight alloy metal

GANDINI

Marcello Gandini was born in 1938. His first job was to repair damaged car bodies, but he went on to design them instead. In the 1960s he worked for the Bertone company. Here he designed the Lamborghini Miura, one of the first **supercars**. This superb car made him famous. Then he designed sports cars for Ferrari, Maserati, Alfa Romeo and Fiat. In 1971 he designed the spectacular Lamborghini Countach.

The flowing lines of Marcello Gandini's Lamborghini Miura.

FERRARI 550 BARCHETTA

- Date production started: 2000
- Where made: Italy
- **Chassis**: tubular
- Engine position: front
- Engine type: 5.5-litre V12
- Power: 485 bhp
- **Acceleration**: 0–60 mph (96 km/h) in 4.4 seconds
- Top speed: 186 mph (299 km/h)

FERRARI

Ferrari is the most famous name in the history of sports cars. Almost every Ferrari model is a classic car. People who love sports cars dream of having their own Ferrari. A few lucky ones do. The man behind the company was Enzo Ferrari. He was born in Italy in 1898. When he was a boy, Enzo went to several motor races. He decided to become a racing driver. He turned out to be good at it and Alfa Romeo gave him a job in their racing team. In the 1920s and 1930s Enzo built and raced cars for Alfa Romeo with great success.

Enzo Ferrari testing an Alfa Romeo racer in 1924.

FERRARI BIRTHDAYS

To celebrate its 40th birthday in 1987, Ferrari built the F40 **supercar**. Its top speed is 200 mph (322 km/h). Ten years later it built the F50 to celebrate its 50th birthday.

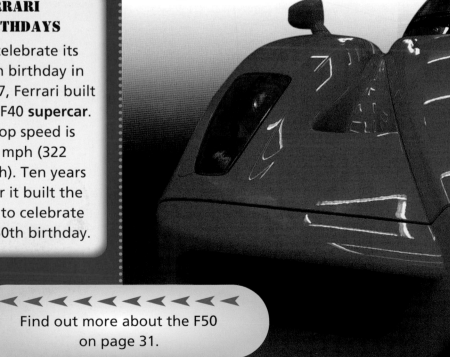

Find out more about the F50 on page 31.

UP TO SPEED fighter ace pilot famous for shooting down enemy aircraft in war

FERRARIS ON THE ROAD

In 1943 Enzo set up a factory at Maranello in Italy. The company's first car was the Ferrari 125 Sport. This was designed to be a racing car as well as a road car. Enzo was always most interested in racing. He said that he sold sports cars to pay for the company's racing teams. Famous Ferrari cars include the Daytona, the Dino and the Testarossa. Enzo's favourite was the 250 GTO. Enzo Ferrari died in 1988. The Ferrari Enzo (below), launched in 2002, is named after him.

The Enzo is the same F1 car driven by Michael Schumacher, but with a body on top.

THE PRANCING HORSE

In 1923 Enzo Ferrari met the parents of Italian World War One **fighter ace** Francesco Baracca. They gave him a badge from their son's fighter squadron. It was a prancing horse that became Ferrari's badge.

A **convertible** version of the Volkswagen, pictured in 1938.

An early Porsche 911. This is the **coupé** version.

PORSCHE

Porsche is one of Germany's leading sports car companies. It is successful on the road and on the track. The company is named after Dr Ferdinand Porsche. He was born in 1875. He quickly became famous as an engineer and test driver. He then worked for the German car maker Daimler. In the 1930s Ferdinand Porsche designed the first Volkswagen. This car later became known as the famous Beetle. The first Porsche sports car was made in 1948. It was based on the Volkswagen and was called the Porsche 356. It featured a rear engine and could do 85 mph (137 km/h).

convertible   car with a roof that can be removed

THE PORSCHE 911

At the 1963 Frankfurt Motor Show, Porsche showed off its new sports car. It was the Porsche 911, one of the greatest sports cars ever. Like the 356, the 911 has a rear engine. But the engine is more powerful, with six **cylinders**. The body was designed by Ferdinand Porsche's son. A **turbocharged** version of the 911 was developed in 1974. There have been many versions of the Porsche 911 since 1963. The shape has gradually changed, but the 911 is still being made.

PORSCHE FACTS

- The Porsche 356 was the first Porsche to win the Le Mans 24 Hour Race.
- 77,361 Porsche 356s were made.
- The Porsche 959 was the first sports car to win the Paris-Dakar Rally.

PORSCHE 911 GT2

- Date production started: 2001
- Where made: Germany
- **Chassis: unitary**
- Engine position: rear
- Engine type: 3.6-litre turbocharged flat 6
- Power: 462 bhp
- **Acceleration**: 0–60 mph (96 km/h) in 4.1 seconds
- Top speed: 196 mph (315 km/h)

unitary chassis   framework that includes a car's side and roof panels, floor and engine compartment

DESIGNING A SUPERCAR

Sports car **manufacturers** build **supercars** to help sell their other sports cars and to make sure they have good racing teams. They want people to like their supercars because it makes people talk about them. A supercar also shows off a company's new technology. Some supercars are made to celebrate important dates in a company's history.

SKETCHY START

Supercars start life as ideas in the heads of company bosses. Then a team of people start work to make the car a reality. A **stylist** takes the ideas and makes lots of rough sketches on paper. After many discussions and new sketches, the stylist works out a final look for the car.

TESTING AND PRODUCTION

Testing is an important part of making a new car. Engineers make and test every part of the new supercar. They make a prototype car to drive to make sure it is safe. They also do **aerodynamic** tests in a wind tunnel.

The Bengal, a concept car displayed by Buick in 2003.

concept   idea
stylist   person who designs the shape of a car

DESIGNING THE CAR

The stylist designs the seats, dashboard and instruments as well as the body. Engineers work out what materials to use for the **chassis** and body. Engineers also decide what engine will power the car and choose a **transmission** and wheels.

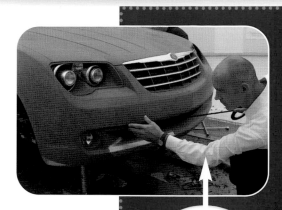

Designer working on a mock-up of a Chrysler Crossfire.

CONCEPT CARS

Finally the first car is built. Now it is time for the public to see the new supercar. It is displayed at one of the top motor shows, such as Paris, Tokyo or Detroit. There is no guarantee that it will be a **production car**. At the moment it is called a **concept** car. If the public like it, a new supercar may go into production. You could be seeing one on the road very soon.

BUGATTI VEYRON

- Date production started: 2004
- Where made: Italy
- Chassis: **unitary**
- Engine position: mid-engined
- Engine type: 8.0-litre twin V8
- Power: 987 bhp
- **Acceleration**: 0–60 mph (96 km/h) in 3.0 seconds
- Top speed: 252 mph (406 km/h)

transmission   machinery that connects a car's engine to its wheels

SPORTS CAR FACTS

WORLD RALLY CHAMPIONS

Year	Driver	Manufacturer
2003	Petter Solberg	Subaru
2002	Marcus Gronhölm	Peugeot
2001	Richard Burns	Subaru
2000	Marcus Gronhölm	Peugeot
1999	Tommi Makinen	Mitsubishi
1998	Tommi Makinen	Mitsubishi

LE MANS WINNERS

Year	Car	Winners
2003	Bentley Exp Speed 8	Tom Kristensen, Guy Smith, Dindo Capello
2002	Audi R8	Frank Biela, Tom Kristensen, Emanuele Pirro
2001	Audi R8	Frank Biela, Tom Kristensen, Emanuele Pirro
2000	Audi R8	Frank Biela, Tom Kristensen, Emanuele Pirro
1999	BMW V12 LMR	Pierluigi Martini, Yannick Dalmas, Joachim Winkelhock
1998	Porsche 911 GT1-98	Allan McNish, Laurent Aiello, Stephane Ortelli

SPORTS CAR ON WATER

The Aquada Sports Amphibian is a sports car that turns into a sports boat at the touch of a button. It has a top speed of 100 mph (160 km/h) on land and 30mph (48 km/h) on water.

FASTEST SUPERCARS

Car	0–60 mph	Year
Bugatti Veyron	3.0 secs	2004
McLaren F1	3.2 secs	1993
Ferrari Enzo	3.6 secs	2002
Pagani Zonda	3.7 secs	2002
Mercedes Benz CLK-GTR	3.8 secs	1998
Dodge Viper	3.9 secs	2003
Noble M12 GTO	3.9 secs	2000
Jaguar XJ220	4.0 secs	1993
Porsche 911 Turbo	4.2 secs	2000
Ferrari Modena	4.3 secs	2000
TVR Tuscan	4.3 secs	2001
Aston Martin Vanquish	4.7 secs	2000
Lotus Elise 111R	4.9 secs	2004
Morgan Aero 8	4.9 secs	2000
Toyota Supra Turbo	5.3 secs	1998
BMW Z4	5.4 secs	2003
Lamborghini Countach	5.6 secs	1982
Mazda RX-8	6.4 secs	2003
Lamborghini Miura	6.7 secs	1971

DAKAR RALLY WINNERS (CAR CATEGORY)

Year	Drivers	Manufacturer
2004	Stephane Peterhansel, Jean-Paul Cottret	Mitsubishi
2003	Hiroshi Masuoka, Andreas Schulz	Mitsubishi
2002	Hiroshi Masuoka, Pascal Maimon	Mitsubishi
2001	Jutta Kleinschmidt, Andreas Schulz	Mitsubishi
2000	Jean-Louis Schlesser, Henri Magne	Renault
1999	Jean-Louis Schlesser, Henri Magne	Renault
1998	Jean-Pierre Fontenay, Gilles Picard	Mitsubishi

ORGANIZATIONS

Ferrari
www.ferrari.it

Porsche
www.uk.porsche.com

Jaguar
www.jaguar.com

Dodge
www.dodge.com

Bugatti
www.bugatti-cars.de

**World Rally
Championship**
www.wrc.com

**International
Automobile
Federation**
www.fia.com

NASCAR
www.nascar.com

BOOKS

Debenham, Ian, *Investigate Racing Cars* (Chrysalis Children's Books, 2002)

Graham, Ian, *Designed for Success: Racing Cars* (Heinemann Library, 2003)

Graham, Ian, *Designed for Success: Sports Cars* (Heinemann Library, 2003)

Johnstone, Michael, *The Need for Speed: Stock Car Racing* (Watts Books, 2002)

Lord, Trevor, *Big Book of Race Cars* (Dorling Kindersley, 2001)

Maynard, C., *Supreme Machines: Racing Cars* (Watts Books, 1999)

WORLD WIDE WEB

If you want to find out more about sports cars you can search the Internet using keywords like these:

Aston Martin cars
Enzo Ferrari
Lamborghini cars
Jaguar sport cars
Jean Bugatti
Porsche cars
supercars
World **Rally**
NASCAR
monocoque chassis
V12 engine

Make your own keywords using headings or words from this book. The search tips opposite will help you to find the most useful websites.

SEARCH TIPS

There are billions of pages on the Internet so it can be difficult to find exactly what you are looking for. If you just type in 'car' on a search engine like Google, you will get a list of millions of web pages. These search skills will help you find useful websites more quickly.

- Use simple keywords, not whole sentences.
- Use two to six keywords in a search.
- Be precise – only use names of people, places or things.
- If you want to find words that go together, put quote marks around them, for example 'world speed record'.
- Use the advanced section of your search engine.
- Use the + sign between keywords to find pages with all these words.

WHERE TO SEARCH

SEARCH ENGINE

Each search engine looks through millions of web pages and lists all sites that match the search words. The best matches are at the top of the list, on the first page. Try **bbc.co.uk/search**

SEARCH DIRECTORY

A search directory is like a library of websites. You can try searching by keyword or subject and browse through the different sites like you look through books on a library shelf. A good example is **yahooligans.com**

GLOSSARY

acceleration how quickly a car speeds up

accelerator foot pedal used to make a car's engine produce more or less power

aerodynamics science of how air flows around moving objects

air scoop one of the holes in a car body that funnels air to cool the brakes

alloy wheels wheels made from lightweight alloy metal

aluminium a strong, lightweight metal

brake horse power (bhp) a measurement of engine power

cam shaft rod that turns to make valves open and close

capacity total space inside all the cylinders of a car engine

carbon fibre very hard, strong, light material

championship series of races that count towards winning a prize

chassis framework that supports a car's body

chicane narrow part of a race track that makes cars slow down

clutch device that is used to change gear

co-driver in rallying, a person who gives the driver information about the road ahead

cooling duct one of the pipes that carries air to an engine to cool it

concept idea

convertible car with a roof that can be removed

coupé sports car with a body that curves gently from the roof to the rear

crankshaft part of an engine that turns and is connected to the transmission

cylinder tube-shaped part of an engine where fuel is burned

deflector device that makes air hitting a car flow to one side

drag force that tries to stop things moving through the air

drop-top car with a fold-down roof

enthusiast person who really enjoys a particular hobby

faired-in word describing headlamps that are built into the shape of a car body

fighter ace pilot famous for shooting down enemy aircraft in war

fixed-head car with a roof that cannot be removed or folded

four-wheel drive vehicle that has all four wheels turned directly by the engine

Formula One type of racing for purpose-built racing cars

friction force that tries to stop surfaces sliding past each other

front-wheel drive vehicle that has its front wheels turned directly by the engine

grand tourer (GT) another name for a coupé

Indy Car type of racing in the USA similar to Formula One

internal combustion what happens when fuel burns inside the engine

kevlar very strong type of fibre

manufacturer company that designs and builds cars

modified changed

monocoque single-piece chassis

NASCAR short for National Association for Stock Car Auto Racing

piston sits inside the cylinder and moves backwards and forwards

production car car built in large numbers for general sale

professional person who gets paid for driving a car

radiator part of a car that cools hot waste from the engine

rally cross-country race

rear-wheel drive vehicle that has its rear wheels turned directly by the engine

rev counter instrument that shows how quickly the engine's crankshaft is turning

revolution one complete turn

roadster two-seater sports car with no roof

roll cage strong cage that protects a driver and passengers if a car rolls over in a crash

spark plug device that makes a spark so that fuel explodes in an engine

speedometer instrument that shows a car's speed

stylist person who designs the shape of a car

supercar sports car with incredible performance

supercharger device that blows air into an engine, driven by the engine

suspension system in a car that absorbs bumps in the road surface

tarmac hard, smooth road covering

transmission machinery that connects a car's engine to its wheels

tuned adjusted to give maximum power

turbocharger device that blows air into an engine, driven by exhaust gases

unitary chassis framework that includes a car's side and roof panels, floor and engine compartment

valve allows movement of a fluid in one direction only

INDEX

aerodynamics 16,
   32, 60
alloy wheels 11, 50
Aston Martin 5, 35, 60

BMW 7, 23, 43
Bugatti cars 33,
   48–49, 57, 60
Bugatti, Ettore 48–49
Bugatti, Jean 49, 60
Buick 56

cam shafts 21
capacity 22, 24, 39
Chevrolet 35
Chrysler 21, 57
co-drivers 45, 47
concept cars 57
convertibles 11, 54
coupés 10–11, 32, 35,
   49, 54

drag 16–17

Farina, Giovan
   Battista 50
Ferrari cars 4, 29, 31,
   35, 43, 48, 50–54, 60
Ferrari, Enzo 35,
   52–53, 60
Fiat 50–51
four-stroke cycle
   20–21
four-wheel drive 14

Formula One 28,
   30–31, 38
friction 26–27
front-wheel drive 14

Gandini, Marcello 51
Ghia, Giacinto 50

Indy Cars 38

Jaguar 4, 29, 34, 48, 60

Lamborghini 4, 29,
   36, 51, 60
Le Mans 5, 42–43,
   48, 55

Mazda 11
McLaren 29–30, 42
Mercedes 29, 33, 39
modified 38, 41, 45
monocoque 15, 18,
   29–31, 39, 61
Morgan 37

NASCAR (National
   Association for
   Stock Car Racing)
   37, 41, 60
Noble 19

Pagani 15
Peugeot 38–39
Pininfarina 31, 50
Porsche cars 22, 43,
   50, 54–55, 60
Porsche, Ferdinand 54

rally cars 14, 44–45, 47
rear-wheel drive 14
Renault 10
roadster 10

safety 7, 18, 26, 42, 46
spark plugs 20–21
speedometer 13
stylists 48–50, 56–57
superchargers 24,
   33, 61
suspensions 26, 31, 47

Toyota 25
transmissions 13–14,
   22, 24–25, 57, 61
turbocharger 24, 61
TVR 19, 25
tyres 4, 24, 26–27,
   38, 41, 44, 46

unitary chassis 10, 18

valves 20–22, 33, 39

World Rally
   Championship 44, 60

Titles in the *Mean Machines* series include:

Hardback   1 844 43164 9

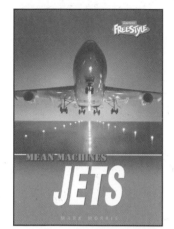

Hardback   1 844 43161 4

Hardback   1 844 43172 X

Hardback   1 844 43174 6

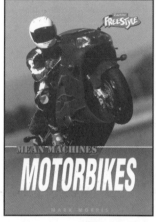

Hardback   1 844 43163 0

Hardback   1 844 43162 2

Hardback   1 844 43173 8

Hardback   1 844 43171 1

Find out about the other titles in this series on our website www.raintreepublishers.co.uk